Introducing Religions

D0512208

Sikhism

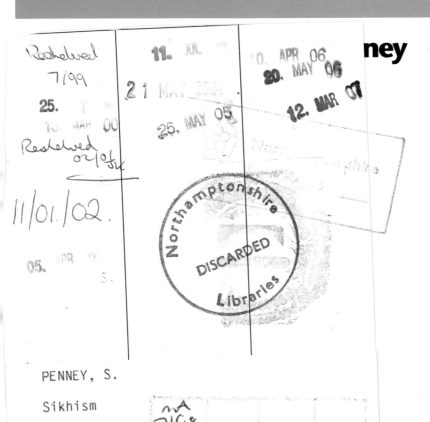

Reshelved 7/99

25.

19. MAR 00

Reshelved 02/02/fk

11/01/02.

05. APR

11. JUL

21 MAY 2004

25. MAY 05

10. APR 06

20. MAY 06

12. MAR 07

Northamptonshire DISCARDED Libraries

PENNEY, S.

Sikhism

7/98

Please return or renew this item by the last date shown.
You may renew items (unless they have been requested
by another customer) by telephoning, writing to or calling
in at any library.   100% recycled paper   BKS 1 (5/95)

80 001 315 940

First published in Great Britain by Heinemann Library,
Halley Court, Jordan Hill, Oxford OX2 8EJ,
a division of Reed Educational & Professional Publishing Ltd

OXFORD FLORENCE PRAGUE MADRID ATHENS MELBOURNE
AUCKLAND KUALA LUMPUR SINGAPORE TOKYO IBADAN
NAIROBI KAMPALA JOHANNESBURG GABORONE
PORTSMOUTH NH (USA) CHICAGO MEXICO CITY SAO PAULO

© Sue Penney 1997

First published 1997

ISBN 0 431 06640 X hardback

01 00 99 98 97
10 9 8 7 6 5 4 3 2 1

ISBN 0 431 06647 7 paperback

01 00 99 98 97
10 9 8 7 6 5 4 3 2 1

British Library Cataloguing in Publication Data

Penney, Sue
  Sikhism. – (Introducing religions)
  1. Sikhism – Juvenile literature
  I. Title
  294.6

Northamptonshire Libraries & Information Service	
Peters	22-Jan-98
C294.6	£5.25

Designed and typeset by Artistix
Illustrated by Gecko Limited. Adapted into colour by Visual Image
Produced by Mandarin Offset
Printed and bound in the UK by Bath Press Colourbooks, Glasgow

Acknowledgements

Thanks are due to Kawal Singh and Liz Powlay for reading and advising on the manuscript.

The publishers would like to thank the following for permission to reproduce photographs:
Andes Press Agency pp. 11, 21, 28, 44; Mohamed Ansar/Impact Photos p. 23; Circa Photo Library pp. 10, 42, 43; Mary Evans Picture Library p. 25; Sally and Richard Greenhill pp. 9, 36; Robert Harding Picture Library p. 26; Judy Harrison/Format Partners pp. 12 (top), 33, 39; The Hutchison Library pp. 6, 12 (below), 18, 22, 40, 41, 47; Christine Osborne Pictures pp. 13, 14, 32, 34, 35, 38, 46; Ann and Bury Peerless pp. 17, 19, 27, 29, 30, 31; Peter Sanders pp. 15, 45.

The publishers would like to thank Twin Studio for permission to reproduce the cover photograph.

Every effort has been made to contact the copyright holders of any material reproduced in this book. Any omissions will be rectified in subsequent printings if notice is given to the publisher.

Contents

MAP: where the main religions began

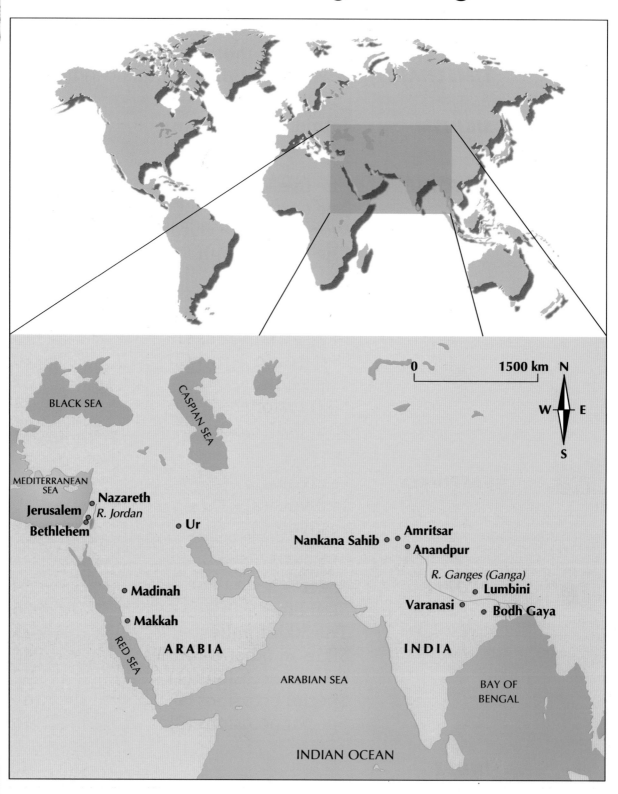

TIMECHART: when the main religions began

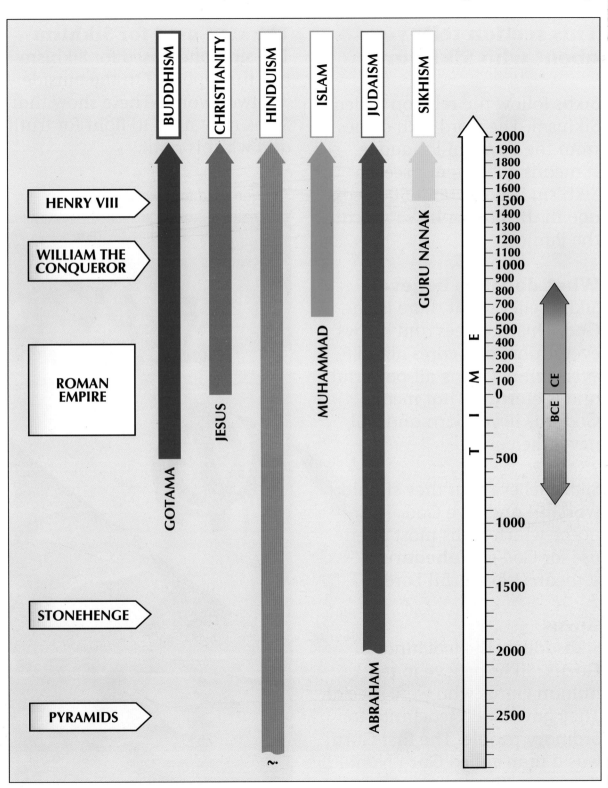

Note about dating systems *In this book dates are not called BC and AD, which is the Christian dating system. The letters BCE and CE are used instead. BCE stands for 'Before the Common Era' and CE stands for 'Common Era'. BCE and CE can be used by people of all religions, Christians too. The year numbers are not changed.*

Introducing Sikhism

This section tells you about who Sikhs are.

Sikhs follow the religion called Sikhism. The word Sikh comes from the **Punjabi** language. It means a learner or seeker. Sikhism began about 500 years ago in the part of India we call the Punjab.

What do Sikhs believe?

Sikhs believe that there is one God. This God sees and knows everything, and cares about everything. God is all-powerful, and is **eternal**. That means God was never born and will never die.

Sikhs believe that they should **worship** and love God. The name which Sikhs most often use for God is **Waheguru**. It means Wonderful Lord.

Gurus

Sikhs follow the teachings of **Gurus**. Sikhs believe in ten human Gurus who were special. They gave God's teachings to ordinary people. The first Guru was a man called Guru Nanak. (See page 16.)

The sign used for Sikhism

The sign often used for Sikhism has three parts. On the outside are two swords. These show that Sikhs may need to fight for truth and what is right.

The sign used for Sikhism

Between the swords is a circle. This reminds Sikhs that there is one God, and God has no beginning and no end, like a circle. In the middle is a two-edged sword called a **khanda**. This is a sign of God's power.

Another sign which Sikhs often use is made from letters. The letters mean 'There is only one God'.

This means, 'There is only one God'.

New words

eternal lasting for ever
Guru religious teacher (for Sikhs, one of ten religious teachers)
khanda two-edged sword
Punjabi Indian language spoken by most Sikhs
Waheguru Sikh name for God
worship pray and give thanks to God

Describing God

Sikhs usually use the name Waheguru for God. Sometimes they use the name Satnam, which means 'eternal reality'. This shows that they believe God has always been real. Sikhs never talk about God as 'He' or 'She'. This is because they believe that God is a spirit, and so is not male or female. They believe that God made people to be male and female, but it is wrong to talk about God as being either of these things. Guru Nanak said that God is 'neither a man nor a woman'.

Guru Nanak also said that God is 'our mother and father'. Sikhs believe that this shows how God cares about everything. They believe that in return people should care about God. Being careful about how they describe God is a way of reminding Sikhs how important God is.

The five Ks

This section tells you about special things Sikhs wear.

All full members of the Sikh religion wear five things which show they are Sikhs. In Punjabi, their names all begin with 'K'. So they are called the five Ks. Wearing the five Ks was begun by the tenth Guru, Guru Gobind Singh.

Kachera

Kachera are short trousers, worn as underwear. They were different from the long loose clothes that people often wore at that time.

Kara

The kara is a narrow bracelet made of steel. Sikhs wear it on their right wrist. It reminds them of God. The bracelet is a circle. Like a circle, God has no beginning and no end. The steel is strong. It reminds Sikhs that they must be strong when they are standing up for what is right.

Kesh

Kesh means hair. Guru Gobind Singh said that it should never be cut. For men, this also means not shaving.

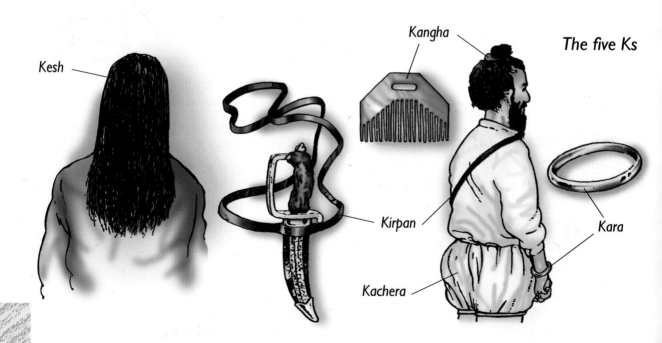

Kesh

Kangha

Kirpan

Kachera

Kara

The five Ks

Kangha

The kangha is a small comb worn in the hair. For Sikhs, being clean and tidy is important. Keeping their hair clean and tidy reminds them that their lives should be tidy and organized, too.

Kirpan

The kirpan is a sword. It reminds Sikhs that they should fight for what is right. It must never be used for attacking people. Most Sikhs today carry a short sword, which is kept in a special case with a strap.

A Sikh boy wearing a turban and the five Ks

The turban

A turban is a long piece of cloth which is wound round the head. It is not one of the five Ks, but wearing it is important for many male and some female Sikhs. Other men in India wear turbans, but they have become a special sign for Sikhs.

A turban is wound round so that it covers the head completely. (See page 27.) It helps to keep a Sikh's uncut hair tidy. Many Sikh families have a turban-tying ceremony for Sikh boys at about the age of ten. This is the age when boys wear a turban for the first time. A Sikh man should not wear any other cap or hat on his head.

The Guru Granth Sahib

This section tells you about the holy book of the Sikhs.

The Guru Granth Sahib is used in all Sikh worship. Weddings take place in front of it, and babies are named using it. It always takes the most important place in the worship room. Having a Guru Granth Sahib is what makes a building a Gurdwara.

The Guru Granth Sahib

The Guru Granth Sahib is a collection of **hymns**. A hymn is a special sort of poem which is used in worship.

Taking the covers off the Guru Granth Sahib

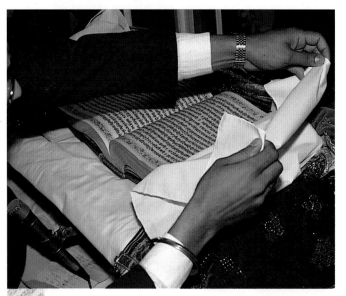

Guru Nanak, the first Guru, wrote 974 hymns in the Guru Granth Sahib. Other hymns were written by other Gurus. There are also some hymns written by holy men who were **Hindus** and **Muslims**. Their ideas were similar to the ideas of the Sikh Gurus. The Guru Granth Sahib was completed by the tenth Guru in 1706. Since then, nothing has been added or taken away.

For nearly 200 years, all copies of the Guru Granth Sahib were carefully written out by hand. In 1852, a group of important Sikhs had a meeting and decided that they would allow copies to be printed for the first time. They also agreed that every copy should be exactly the same.

This is the reason why today every copy of the Guru Granth Sahib has the same number of pages – 1430. A hymn in one copy is always found on the same page in any other copy.

Gutkas

Some Sikhs have a copy of the Guru Granth Sahib at home.

Kangha

The kangha is a small comb worn in the hair. For Sikhs, being clean and tidy is important. Keeping their hair clean and tidy reminds them that their lives should be tidy and organized, too.

Kirpan

The kirpan is a sword. It reminds Sikhs that they should fight for what is right. It must never be used for attacking people. Most Sikhs today carry a short sword, which is kept in a special case with a strap.

A Sikh boy wearing a turban and the five Ks

The turban

A turban is a long piece of cloth which is wound round the head. It is not one of the five Ks, but wearing it is important for many male and some female Sikhs. Other men in India wear turbans, but they have become a special sign for Sikhs.

A turban is wound round so that it covers the head completely. (See page 27.) It helps to keep a Sikh's uncut hair tidy. Many Sikh families have a turban-tying ceremony for Sikh boys at about the age of ten. This is the age when boys wear a turban for the first time. A Sikh man should not wear any other cap or hat on his head.

The Guru Granth Sahib

This section tells you about the holy book of the Sikhs.

The Guru Granth Sahib is used in all Sikh worship. Weddings take place in front of it, and babies are named using it. It always takes the most important place in the worship room. Having a Guru Granth Sahib is what makes a building a Gurdwara.

The Guru Granth Sahib

The Guru Granth Sahib is a collection of **hymns**. A hymn is a special sort of poem which is used in worship.

Taking the covers off the Guru Granth Sahib

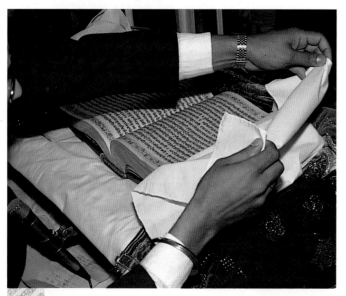

Guru Nanak, the first Guru, wrote 974 hymns in the Guru Granth Sahib. Other hymns were written by other Gurus. There are also some hymns written by holy men who were **Hindus** and **Muslims**. Their ideas were similar to the ideas of the Sikh Gurus. The Guru Granth Sahib was completed by the tenth Guru in 1706. Since then, nothing has been added or taken away.

For nearly 200 years, all copies of the Guru Granth Sahib were carefully written out by hand. In 1852, a group of important Sikhs had a meeting and decided that they would allow copies to be printed for the first time. They also agreed that every copy should be exactly the same.

This is the reason why today every copy of the Guru Granth Sahib has the same number of pages – 1430. A hymn in one copy is always found on the same page in any other copy.

Gutkas

Some Sikhs have a copy of the Guru Granth Sahib at home.

Reading the Guru Granth Sahib

Sikhs believe that it is so important that it should not be kept with other books. It should have a room of its own. This room then becomes a Gurdwara, because the Guru Granth Sahib is there. All Sikhs have smaller books called **Gutkas**. Gutkas contain hymns taken from the Guru Granth Sahib, and other prayers which Sikhs say every day. Sikhs treat Gutkas with great care, too.

New words

Gutka book containing the most important Sikh hymns and the daily prayers

Hindus followers of the religion of Hinduism

hymn kind of poem used in worship

Muslims followers of the religion of Islam

How to treat the Guru Granth Sahib

When it is being used, the Guru Granth Sahib is put on the takht, the special throne at the front of the worship room. While it is open, there is always somebody sitting behind it to take care of it. When it is closed, it is covered with special cloths.

If the Gurdwara is large enough, the Guru Granth Sahib is put away at night in a room of its own. There is a ceremony to 'put it to bed' and another one to return it to the worship room the next morning. Carrying it is a great honour. It is always carried so that it is on the person's head. Sikhs treat it so carefully because they believe it is the word of God.

Guru Nanak

This section tells you about the first Sikh Guru.

Nanak was born in 1469 CE in a small village in India. The stories say that he was a special baby.

When he was a child, he was very interested in religion. His family were Hindu, but Nanak did not agree with everything that Hinduism taught.

When he grew up, Nanak went to work in an office. The people in the office were Muslims. Nanak talked to them about what they believed, too.

When he was about 30 years old, Nanak disappeared.

His friends thought that he must have drowned in the river. After three days, he came back to the village. Everyone was very pleased that he was not dead.

Nanak told the people that he had had a **vision** in which he had seen God. God had told him to teach people that they should live in a truthful way. They should treat all people as God's children.

After this time, Nanak was called Guru Nanak. He spent many years travelling around India and other countries teaching people.

This map shows the four journeys which Guru Nanak made.

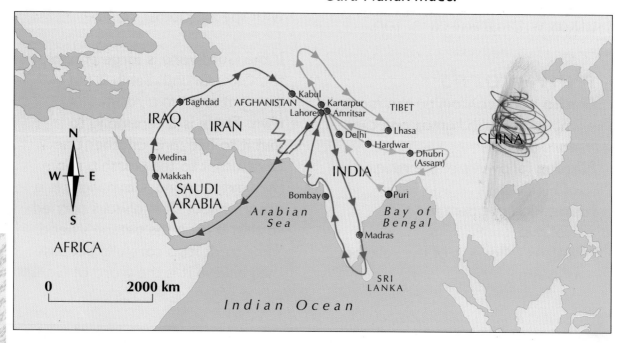

Guru Nanak

Before Guru Nanak died, he chose Lehna to be the next Guru. He gave him a new name. He called him Angad. Angad means 'part of me'. Guru Nanak died in 1539 CE.

New words

meditate think deeply, especially about religion

vision special dream, usually to do with religion

When he was an old man, Guru Nanak settled down in a village in northern India. A group of people came to live nearby. They wanted to learn more about what Guru Nanak was teaching. They became known as Sikhs because Sikh means 'someone who wants to learn'.

These people met for worship, and **meditated** together. Guru Nanak taught the people about God and about the right way to live. One of the men who came to learn was called Lehna.

What Guru Nanak taught

There is only one God. Worship and pray only to the one God.

Different religions are different paths to the same one God. All humans are children of the same one God.

Remember God, work hard and help others.

Men and women are all equal before God.

Be kind to people, animals and birds.

Always speak the truth.

Other Sikh Gurus (1)

This section tells you about the three Gurus who came after Guru Nanak.

After Guru Nanak there were nine other Gurus. Sikhs say that all the Gurus thought in the same way. They say that they were like candles that have all been lit from the same flame. Each of the Gurus helped to make the new religion of Sikhism more organized.

Guru Angad (1539–52)

Guru Angad was chosen by Guru Nanak. His most important work was writing down the hymns which Guru Nanak had written.

In those days, many people could not read or write. Guru Angad wanted to write down the hymns, but there was a problem. The people spoke Punjabi, but no one had ever written it down. Guru Angad worked out a way of writing Punjabi. It was called **Gurmukhi**. It is the language in which all the Sikh holy books are written.

Guru Amar Das (1552–74)

Before he died, Guru Angad chose one of his Sikhs as the next Guru. He was called Guru Amar Das. He chose 22 Sikh men and women to be **missionaries** and tell people about the teachings of Guru Nanak.

Guru Amar Das asked all Sikhs to come to a big meeting twice a year, in the town where the Guru lived. This meant that he could meet them all himself. Gura Amar Das also continued Guru Nanak's teaching about how important it was that everyone should eat together.

The Guru Granth Sahib is written in Gurmukhi.

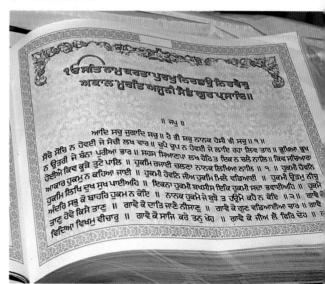

The Golden Temple at Amritsar

Guru Ram Das (1574-81)

Guru Ram Das was chosen by Guru Amar Das. He decided that Sikhs should have a city which could be the centre of their faith. So he began building the city of Amritsar, which is in the Punjab in northern India.

Guru Ram Das also wrote the Sikh wedding hymns which Sikhs still use at their weddings.

New words
Gurmukhi written form of the Punjabi language
missionary someone who tells other people about their religion

Choosing a Guru

There is a story that Guru Nanak's sons thought one of them should be the next Guru. But Guru Nanak set them a test. He dropped a cup into a ditch full of muddy water. Then he asked for someone to go and get it.

His sons refused. They thought the Guru's sons were too good to do a job like that. But Lehna (Guru Angad) jumped into the water straight away without even being asked. Guru Nanak said that he should be the next Guru. He had shown that he knew caring for other people was important.

Other Sikh Gurus (2)

This section tells you about the later Sikh Gurus.

Guru Arjan (1581–1606)

Guru Arjan was the son of Guru Ram Das. He carried on the building at Amritsar begun by his father. He built a Gurdwara in the middle of a lake there. This is now the Golden Temple. It is the most important building in the Sikh religion.

Guru Har Gobind (1606–44)

Guru Har Gobind was Guru Arjan's son. He showed the Sikhs that they needed to fight for what they believed. Because of this, he was put in prison.

Then the ruler of India decided to let the Guru go free. The Guru refused to leave until 52 Hindu rulers who were also in the prison were allowed out, too. Sikhs remember this story every year (see page 33).

Guru Har Rai (1644–61)

Guru Har Rai was Guru Har Gobind's grandson. He opened hospitals where medicine and treatment were given free to all.

Guru Har Krishan (1661-4)

Guru Har Krishan was the son of Guru Har Rai. Even though he was very young, he cared about other people. He died when he was only eight years old, after he had helped to look after people suffering from smallpox.

Guru Tegh Bahadur (1664–75)

Guru Tegh Bahadur was Gur Har Gobind's son. He was killed by the country's rulers because he refused to give up what he believed. His story is on page 30.

Guru Gobind Singh (1675–1708)

Guru Gobind Singh began the **Khalsa**. Khalsa means the pure ones. It is the name for Sikhs who are full members of the religion (see page 22). Before Guru Gobind Singh died, he said that he was not going to choose a new human Guru. From then on, the Sikhs' Guru would be their holy book. This is why it is called the Guru Granth Sahib.

New word

Khalsa full members of the Sikh religion

Guru Gobind Singh

How Guru Gobind Singh chose the Guru Granth Sahib

When Guru Gobind Singh was dying, he asked to be taken to the room where the holy book was kept. At that time the holy book was called the Adi Granth, which means 'first book'. Guru Gobind Singh bowed his head in front of it to show respect. Then he spoke to the people with him.

He said: 'My spirit lives on in the Khalsa and the Guru Granth Sahib. Obey the Guru Granth Sahib. Let anyone who wishes to meet me search its hymns.' He had shown the Sikhs that in future their Guru should be the Guru Granth Sahib. Granth means 'a big book'. Sahib is a word used to show respect.

21

The Khalsa

This section tells you about how the Khalsa began.

What is the Khalsa?

The Khalsa is the name given to Sikhs who are full members of the Sikh religion. The name Khalsa means 'the pure ones'.

The Khalsa was begun by Guru Gobind Singh in 1699. He said that being a member of the Khalsa was more important than anything else. He told the people to do two things to show that they were members.

The first thing people had to do was to drink **amrit** from the same bowl. Amrit is a mixture of sugar and water. In those days people who came from different groups or religions never ate or drank together. Drinking the amrit together showed that they cared more about being Sikhs than they did about where they came from.

The other thing people had to do was share a name. Guru Gobind Singh said that all men should take the name of **Singh**. Singh means lion.

These men are dressed like the Panj Piare.

All the women should take the name of **Kaur**. Kaur means princess. People who share the same name are part of the same family, so sharing these names shows that all Sikhs are part of the family of Sikhism. Since that day, all Sikhs have used these names as part of their own name.

The amrit ceremony

The amrit ceremony is the special ceremony where people join the Khalsa. Apart from the people who are joining, only people who are already members may take part. Everyone wears the five Ks.

The ceremony is led by five people, to remember the five men who offered to give their lives to Guru Gobind Singh. One of the five leaders repeats the duties which members of the Khalsa must keep. There are prayers and readings from the Guru Granth Sahib.

The people who are joining, kneel on their right knee. They drink some amrit, then some is sprinkled on their eyes, hair and hands. There are more prayers, then everyone shares karah parshad. After this ceremony, Sikhs are expected to keep all the duties of the religion.

Preparing for the amrit ceremony

New words
amrit special mixture of sugar and water
amrit ceremony ceremony in which people become members of the Khalsa
Kaur princess
Singh lion

How the Khalsa began

Guru Gobind Singh called a meeting of all the Sikhs. He asked if there was anyone who was ready to die for what they believed. No one answered. He asked this question two more times. One man came forward. Guru Gobind Singh took the man into his tent. Then he came out with his sword covered in blood! He asked the question again. Another man came forward. The same thing happened. Altogether five men were taken away.

Then the Guru went into his tent and came back with all five men. The Guru called them the five beloved ones (Panj Piare), and said they would be the first members of the Khalsa.

Festivals (1)

This section tells you about two of the most important Sikh festivals.

The most important Sikh festivals remember the birth or the death of a Guru. In Punjabi they are called **Gurpurbs**.

The most important part of a Gurpurb is a reading of the Guru Granth Sahib from beginning to end without stopping. This is called an **Akhand Path**.

Akhand Path

An Akhand Path takes about 48 hours.

It is always timed to end early in the morning of the day of the festival. While the reading is going on, Sikhs make a special effort to go to the gurdwara. They listen and meditate. Langar is always served as the reading is taking place.

Guru Nanak's birthday

Sikhs all over the world celebrate the birthday of Guru Nanak every year. There are often processions through the streets. Five people usually lead the procession, to remind Sikhs of the five men who were the first to join the Khalsa.

Reading the Guru Granth Sahib at an Akhand Path

A Gurpurb procession

The most important procession is in the town of Patna in India. This is the town where the Guru was born.

New words
Akhand Path non-stop reading of the Guru Granth Sahib
Gurpurb festival in honour of a Guru

The five wear yellow robes with a wide blue belt, and yellow turbans, because this is what the first five men wore.

Next in the procession comes a lorry or open truck which carries the Guru Granth Sahib on its throne. This is beautifully decorated with flowers and banners. The people in the procession sing hymns from the Guru Granth Sahib. People watching the procession are often given sweets to remember that Guru Nanak said all people should be able to eat together.

The birthday of Guru Gobind Singh
This Gurpurb takes place in December or January. It is celebrated in the same way as the birthday of Guru Nanak.

How an Akhand Path is organized

An Akhand Path is a reading of the Guru Granth Sahib all the way through. The reading can be done by any Sikh who can read Gurmukhi well enough to be able to read it clearly in front of lots of people. People take it in turns, but no one ever reads for more than two hours at a time. This is so that they do not get tired. There is always a reserve reader in case someone is ill.

Before going to the Gurdwara, the reader has a bath, and before starting to read they wash their hands. This is to make sure that they are clean to touch the Guru Granth Sahib, and because they think it is so important.

Festivals (2)

This section tells you about the Gurpurbs which remember the martyrdom of two Sikh Gurus.

The martyrdom of Guru Arjan

Guru Arjan was the first Sikh to be killed because of what he believed. Someone who dies because of their religion is called a **martyr**, so their death is called a martyrdom. Guru Arjan was killed because he refused to change his religion to the religion of the country's ruler.

A Gurpurb procession, remembering Guru Tegh Bahadur

Sikhs remember Guru Arjan's death in June every year. Like most Gurpurbs, it is remembered with processions.

The martyrdom of Guru Tegh Bahadur

Guru Tegh Bahadur's death is remembered in November or December every year. It is especially important in Delhi, the capital of India. This is where he was killed. There is a beautiful Gurdwara at the place where he died. Sikhs go there to worship as part of the Gurpurb.

In India at that time Hindus and Sikhs were being killed.

This was because they would not change their religion. Important Hindus came to see Guru Tegh Bahadur, to ask his advice. The Guru said everyone should be able to worship in the way they felt was right. He went to speak to the Emperor (the ruler of India), who offered the Guru all sorts of good things if he would change his religion. But the Guru refused. The Emperor ordered that the Guru should have his head cut off.

This Gurdwara was built where Guru Tegh Bahadur was killed.

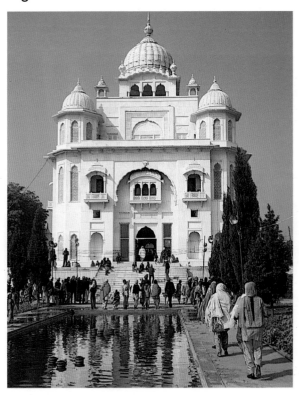

Sikhs believe that this was very important. If Guru Tegh Bahadur had given in, Hindus as well as Sikhs would have had to give up what they believed.

New word

martyr someone who dies for what they believe

Guru Tegh Bahadur

There is a Sikh story which shows that even when Guru Tegh Bahadur was a baby, he was always unusual. The story says that when Tegh Bahadur was born, he was taken to his father, Guru Har Gobind. Guru Har Gobind always wore two swords. This was to show that Sikhs need to fight in two ways – they need to fight for what is right as well as for religious truth.

When Guru Har Gobind took his son in his arms, the baby reached out and held on to one of the swords. This is why his father chose the name Tegh Bahadur, which means 'master of the sword'.

Festivals (3)

This section tells you about the Sikh festivals called melas.

Melas means fairs. There are many melas in different towns in India, celebrating things which happened there. This section looks at two important melas which are celebrated all over the world.

Baisakhi

Baisakhi is a spring festival. It falls on 13 or 14 April. It is a popular time for holding the amrit ceremony.

This is because Baisakhi remembers the time when Guru Gobind Singh began the Khalsa in 1699. (See pages 22–3.)

At Baisakhi there are services in the Gurdwara. The services begin soon after dawn. These may last all day, with people coming and going, leaving when they have stayed as long as they can.

The langar is served all day. There are readings from the Guru Granth Sahib, and readings which remind people of the first Baisakhi and how important it was.

Replacing the Nishan Sahib at Baisakhi

Lighting candles at Divali

Sikhs remember it as the time when Guru Har Gobind was released from prison in 1619. The people in Amritsar were so pleased to see him that they lit lamps in every house to welcome him home.

Like other festivals, Divali is often celebrated with bonfires and firework displays.

New word
mela 'fair' – Sikh festival

At Baisakhi the Nishan Sahib is always changed. This is the Sikh flag which flies outside every Gurdwara. It is taken down, and the flagpole is cleaned. The yellow covers for the flagpole and flag are replaced.

Divali
Divali means festival of lights. It takes place in October or November. It is an important festival for Hindus as well as Sikhs, but they celebrate it in different ways.

A Divali story

At Divali, Sikhs remember that Guru Har Gobind cared about others. The Emperor said he could leave prison, but the Guru said that 52 Hindu princes must be allowed to go, too. The Emperor said that only the princes who could hold onto the Guru's cloak could go, and he must leave through a narrow gate. It was only wide enough for one man. The Guru had long cords fastened to his cloak, so everyone could hold on. All the princes were freed.

Sewa

This section tells you about how Sikhs believe they should help other people.

Sewa is a very important idea for Sikhs. It means service – helping others. Sikhs believe that helping others is part of the way they can worship God.

Sewa is not just helping other Sikhs. The important thing is to offer help to anyone who needs it, no matter who they are.

Sewa may mean giving money to help people who are very poor. Guru Gobind Singh said that if they could, Sikhs should give one-tenth of any money they have earned so that it can be used to help other people. But Sikhs know that this is not always possible. Also, for people who have a lot of money, giving some of it away may not mean very much. Giving their time may be much harder.

There are many jobs which can be part of sewa. Cleaning the Gurdwara, for example, or helping to cook or serve the langar.

Talking to people about what they believe about God can also be part of sewa, but Sikhs do not persuade anyone to become a Sikh. They think it is important that everyone serves God in the way they believe is right.

Medicine
Sewa can also mean helping to look after people who are ill. Sikhs have always believed that caring for people who are ill is important. Guru Nanak spent a lot of his time with people who were ill, and so did many of the other Gurus.

Serving the langar

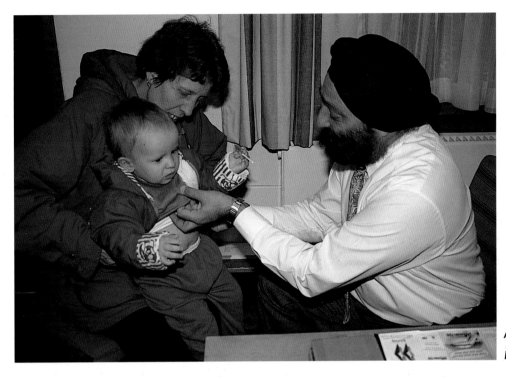

A Sikh doctor in Britain

The eighth Guru, Guru Har Krishan, died because he was helping to look after people who had smallpox. Many Sikhs today become doctors or nurses. In India, where most Sikhs live, many people are too poor to pay for medical care.

Some Indian Gurdwaras have special clinics where people can go to be given free treatment and medicines.

New word
sewa service – helping others

Why care about other people?

Sikhs believe that caring for everyone is an important part of their religion. They believe God loves everyone in exactly the same way, so no one is better than anyone else.

They also believe that you can only love God if you love other people.

Sikhism teaches that all people should be treated equally. There is a story that the third Guru, Guru Amar Das, was visited by the Emperor. The Emperor was very important, but Guru Amar Das still expected him to sit on the floor and eat the langar in the same way as everyone else.

Sikh life

This section tells you about some of the ways in which being a Sikh affects people's lives.

Everyday life

All Sikhs who are members of the Khalsa promise to try to live so that they are as much like the Gurus as possible. This means that they should work hard and earn their living honestly. They should not do any jobs which might hurt other people. Gambling and stealing are forbidden, and so is having affairs.

Sikhs should not take any drugs except proper medicines. They should not drink alcohol or smoke or chew tobacco.

Sikhism does not have strict laws about food, except that no Sikh will eat meat from an animal which has been killed in a way they think is cruel. Many Sikhs do not eat beef, because they do not want to upset Hindus, who believe that cows are holy.

Many Sikhs spend time every day meditating and reading the holy books. The Guru Granth Sahib has been translated into several other languages.

A Gurmukhi class at a Gurdwara

How to tie a turban

But many Sikhs choose to learn Gurmukhi so that they can read it in the language in which it was written.

Turbans

Today, wearing a turban is an important way of showing that someone is a Sikh. It has become a part of what Sikh men wear. A turban is a piece of material about five metres long which is wound around the head.

In India, important people once wore them as a sign that they were powerful. Guru Gobind Singh started to wear one to show that the Sikhs were powerful. Other Sikhs copied him. Sikh men should not wear anything else on their head.

The story of Bhai Lalo

Sikhs tell this story to show why you should live your life carefully. Guru Nanak once chose to visit a poor man called Bhai Lalo. A rich man was upset that Guru Nanak had not visited him instead.

Guru Nanak went to the rich man's house, and picked up a piece of bread. He squeezed it and drops of blood came out. Then he squeezed a piece of bread from Bhai Lalo's house. Drops of milk came out. Guru Nanak said that this showed that Bhai Lalo was honest, even though he was poor. The rich man had made his money by being unkind to other people.

The Sikh family

This section tells you about the way Sikhs live as a family.

In India, where many Sikh families come from, most people live in **extended families**. This means that the family all live together or near to one another. Cousins know each other as well as their brothers and sisters.

Sikhs believe that families are very important. They say that the best way for children to learn about the religion is for them to be taught about it at home, and learn from older relations. Children are taught that they must be polite to older people, and respect their opinions.

Arranged marriages

Sikhs have always believed that part of the duty of the parents is to help their son or daughter choose a wife or husband. This is called an **arranged marriage**.

Marriage joins two families as well as the two people, so it is important that the person chosen is suitable. Years ago, things were very strict, and a couple would not meet before their wedding day. Today, a young person may suggest someone they know and like. They usually meet at least a few times before their wedding. A Sikh couple must agree to their marriage, or it cannot take place.

A Sikh family in Britain

Women can lead worship.

Women in Sikhism

Guru Nanak said that women were just as good as men, and they should be treated in the same way. In those days, this was not usual. There are stories in Sikh history about women soldiers who have fought in battles for the Sikh religion.

In the Gurdwara, men and women are treated the same. They take part in the same ceremonies, and women may become Granthis and lead worship in the Gurdwara. Karah parshad and the langar are served and eaten by men and women together.

New words

arranged marriage marriage in which the partner is chosen or suggested by relations

extended family grandparents, cousins and other relations, living as one family

Teachings about women

At the time of the Gurus, most people thought that women were not as good as men. They were like possessions belonging to a family. When they married, they were given to another family. The Gurus' teachings about women were different.

Apart from Guru Har Krishan, who died when he was a child, all of them were married. This shows that they believed marriage and the family were important. Guru Nanak said that even the most powerful man had once been a baby with a mother, so women should be treated well. This is why Sikhism says that men and women should be treated equally.

Special occasions (3)

This section tells you about what happens when a Sikh dies.

What do Sikhs believe about death?

Sikhs believe that when you die, your **soul** moves on to another body. This cycle of dying and being born again happens over and over again. It goes on until, with God's help, you become close enough to God to break out of the cycle. Then you can go and live with God forever. Guru Nanak said that this belief explains why life can sometimes seem unfair. Things you have done in lives you have lived before can follow you.

This can make a difference to what happens to you in this life.

Believing this makes a difference to what Sikhs believe about death. They say that it is like going to sleep. You go to sleep when you are tired, and wake up ready for another day. In the same way, you die, and are born again to a new life.

Of course, friends and relations are sad that the person they love is not with them any more. But Sikhism teaches them to remember that the person has gone on to another life.

Sikh funerals

After a Sikh has died, their body is washed and dressed in the five Ks. Then it is wrapped in a white sheet. Sikhs are always cremated, and the **funeral** takes place as soon as possible after death.

In India the body is placed on a special fire in the open air. Male relatives help to carry the body and lift it onto the fire. In Western countries, it is taken to a **crematorium**, and male relatives help to carry the coffin.

A Sikh funeral in Britain

46

The most important prayer at the funeral is the **Sohila**. This is the same prayer that Sikhs say every night. It reminds Sikhs that death is like sleep.

Male relatives help to carry the coffin

After the body has been burned, the ashes are scattered on a river or the sea. Sikhs do not put up gravestones. They say that a person should be remembered for the good things they have done in their life.

Guru Nanak's death

There is a story that when Guru Nanak was dying, Sikh friends who had been Hindus and Muslims came to see him. Hindus always cremate people who have died. Muslims always bury them. The Hindus wanted to burn Guru Nanak's body. The Muslims wanted him to say that it could be buried. Guru Nanak said they should cover his body with a cloth, then the Hindus should put flowers at one side, Muslims the other. The people whose flowers were still fresh in the morning could choose what to do.

Guru Nanak died, and his friends did as he said. In the morning, all the flowers were still fresh, but the body had gone! Sikhs say this story shows the soul is far more important than the body.

New words

crematorium place where dead bodies are burned
funeral service to remember someone who has died
Sohila Sikh night-time prayer
soul spirit which lives on after death

Index